STARGAZERS' GUIDES

Can We Travel to the Stars?

Space Flight and Space Exploration

Andrew Solway

www.heinemann.co.uk/library
Visit our website to find out more information about Heinemann Library books.

To order:
☎ Phone 44 (0) 1865 888066
📄 Send a fax to 44 (0) 1865 314091
💻 Visit the Heinemann Bookshop at www.heinemann.co.uk/library to browse our catalogue and order online.

First published in Great Britain by Heinemann Library, Halley Court, Jordan Hill, Oxford OX2 8EJ, part of Harcourt Education. Heinemann is a registered trademark of Harcourt Education Ltd.

Editorial: Nancy Dickmann and Sarah Chappelow
Design: Richard Parker and Tinstar Design
Illustrations: Jeff Edwards
Picture Research: Erica Newbery and Kay Altwegg
Production: Camilla Crask

Originated by Chroma Graphics (Oversea) Pte. Ltd.
Printed in China by WKT Company Limited

10 digit ISBN: 0 431 18190 X
13 digit ISBN: 978 0 431 18190 5
10 09 08 07 06
10 9 8 7 6 5 4 3 2 1

British Library Cataloguing in Publication Data
Solway, Andrew
Can we travel to the stars?
– (Stargazer guides)
629.4
A full catalogue record for this book is available from the British Library.

Acknowledgements
The publishers would like to thank the following for permission to reproduce photographs: Corbis pp. **32**, **33**; Galaxy pp. **4** (Y. Hirose), **5** (Andrew Stewart), **7** (Nigel Evans), **25** (Jhu/NASA), **38** (NASA); Getty Images/ Photodisc pp. **14**, **30**, **34**; NASA pp. **10** (Jpl), **19** (Msfc), **20** (Jsc), **21** (Hq-Grin); Science Photo Library pp. **9** (David Nunuk), **11** (NASA), **12** (UIT Science Team/NASA), **15** (Max-Planck-Institute For Radio Astronomy), **16** (NASA), **17** (NASA), **22** (NASA), **23** (European Space Agency), **24** (Peter Ryan), **26** (NASA), **27** (NASA), **28** (Novosti), **31** (NASA), **35** (NASA), **36**, **37** (David A. Hardy), **39** (Christian Darkin), **40** (European Southern Observatory), **41** (Roger Harris/Science Photo Library And Victor Habbick Visions), **43** (Frank Zullo).

Cover image of space craft reproduced with permission of the Science Photo Library.

The publishers would like to thank Dr. Geza Gyuk of the Adler Planetarium in Chicago for his assistance in the preparation of this book.

Every effort has been made to contact copyright holders of any material reproduced in this book. Any omissions will be rectified in subsequent printings if notice is given to the publishers.

The paper used to print this book comes from sustainable resources.

Disclaimer
All the internet addresses (URLs) given in this book were valid at the time of going to press. However, due to the dynamic nature of the Internet, some addresses may have changed, or sites may have ceased to exist since publication. While the author and publishers regret any inconvenience this may cause readers, no responsibility for any such changes can be accepted by either the author or the publishers.

Contents

Words appearing in the text in bold, **like this**, are explained in the Glossary.

Can we travel to the stars?

On a clear, dark night, the stars can seem very close. It feels as if you could get in a plane and fly up to them. But of course, the stars are not close at all, they are very far away. It would take over 100,000 years to reach the closest stars, travelling at the speed of our fastest rockets.

Every one of the stars in this picture is immensely far away from Earth.

HOT NEWS:
The fastest spaceship

The fastest humans have ever travelled was in 1969, when the spacecraft *Apollo 10* flew round the Moon. On the return journey astronauts Thomas Stafford, John W. Young and Eugene Cernan flew at a speed of 39,937 km/h (24,816 mph).

If people do manage to fly to other stars, they may find other planets where humans could live.

Steps to the stars

At the moment we cannot travel to the stars. But how far have we got? People have travelled to the Moon, which is the first step of the journey. And we have sent unmanned spacecraft (space probes) out to the edges of the **Solar System** – a second step on the journey.

Another step is to know about the stars before we go there. Astronomers have been studying the stars and planets for many years. They have named hundreds of stars, and watched how they move. Since telescopes were invented about 400 years ago, we have been able to see many more stars. In the last 100 years or so, astronomers have also had special instruments such as **spectroscopes** for looking at the colours of stars. These instruments have helped us to find out what stars are made of.

Why go there?

Humans can never resist a challenge. We do not know what we might find among the stars, but wouldn't it be great to find out? We might find other planets like ours, where people could live. We might even find other living things. Imagine being able to meet aliens!

People have travelled to the Moon, and now there are plans to fly to Mars. Who knows? In 100 years time, we could be well on our way to the stars …

Looking at the stars

Humans have watched the stars for thousands of years. In early times, people saw the sky as a place where gods lived, or where people went to live after they died. People studied the stars and planets to find out what the gods were doing, or to get advice from their **ancestors**.

Seeing faraway things nearby

In 1608, three different spectacle-makers in the Netherlands all claimed to have made the first telescope. Their telescopes were tubes with a lens at either end, and they magnified things about three times. News of the invention quickly spread, and in 1609 the Italian scientist Galileo heard about it. He soon made a telescope that magnified eight times, then a better one that could magnify twenty times. Within a few months he had made important discoveries. He worked out the height of the mountains on the Moon, and discovered four moons **orbiting** (going round) the planet Jupiter.

This telescope is not the same type that Galileo originally built, it was developed just a little later. It is the basis for all other astronomical refracting telescopes (telescopes that use lenses to **focus** the light).

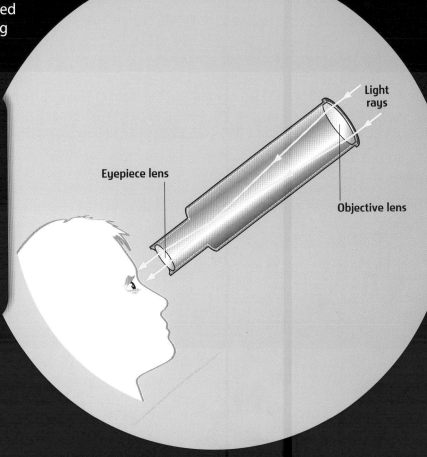

Light rays

Eyepiece lens

Objective lens

The telescope race

It was not long before other people were improving on the basic telescope design. At first, astronomers built longer and longer telescopes to get better magnification. The biggest of these telescopes were over 40 metres (132 feet) long. But the lenses of these telescopes were still very small, and the tube was thin. The wind made the tube bend, and when this happened the telescope did not work. The best practical telescopes from this time magnified about 100 times.

Although telescopes using lenses continued to be built, in the 18th century a new kind of telescope was developed that had definite advantages.

TRY IT YOURSELF:
Following in Galileo's footsteps

If you have a pair of binoculars, they will probably magnify eight or ten times, which is about the same as Galileo's early telescope. Use the binoculars to look at the Moon when it is three-quarters full. Look at the line where the dark and light parts of the Moon meet. You should see strong shadows on the surface. The shadows are caused by mountains and craters. Galileo measured the size of these shadows, and used the measurements to work out the height of the mountains.

The Lowell Observatory in Arizona, USA, has one of the biggest refracting telescopes in the world. The main lens is 60 centimetres (24 inches) across.

All done with mirrors

The new kind of telescope was first made by the great English scientist Sir Isaac Newton in 1668. It was called a reflecting telescope, because instead of focusing light with lenses, it used mirrors.

Newton's telescope

Newton did many studies with light. He was the first person to show that white light can be split into a rainbow of colours using a **prism**. Newton realised that if he used fat lenses in a telescope to get better magnification, the lenses would split some of the white light into many colours. This would produce coloured rings around the image.

The telescope that Newton built had a large curved mirror that magnified the image of what it was pointed at. It focused light onto a flat mirror in the centre of the telescope, which reflected the image into an eyepiece. His telescope was only 15 centimetres (6 inches) long, but it magnified about 40 times. A refracting telescope would need to be at least 90 centimetres (3 feet) long to achieve the same magnification.

In Newton's design of a reflecting telescope, the curved mirror brings the light beams together at the focal point (f). The flat mirror sends the beams into the eyepiece, which magnifies the image for the viewer.

Big reflectors

Newton's telescope did not become popular straight away, but in the 18th century the English astronomer Sir William Herschel built a series of large reflector telescopes. He used these telescopes to make many new discoveries.

In the 19th and 20th centuries reflecting telescopes continued to get bigger. The main, curved mirror grew and grew. The biggest single-mirror reflecting telescopes have mirrors over 8 metres (26 feet) in diameter.

The twin Keck telescopes in Hawaii are among the world's largest reflecting telescopes. Each has a mirror made up of 36 separate hexagonal (6-sided) pieces. The segments work together as if they are a single mirror 10 metres (nearly 33 feet) across.

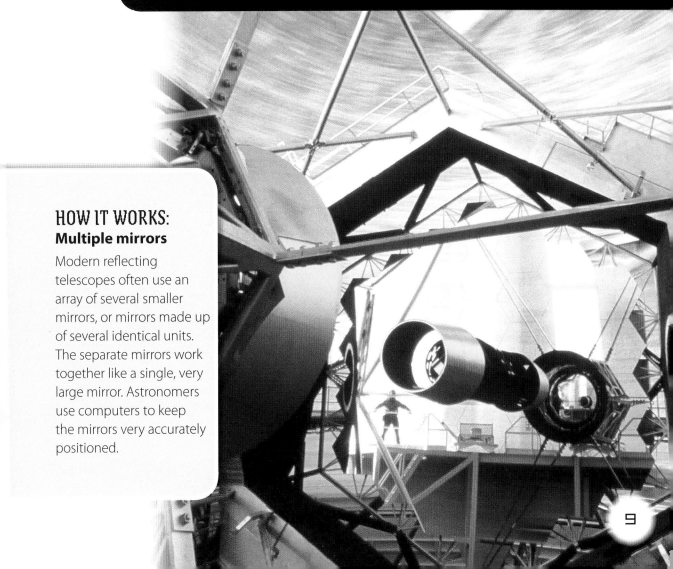

HOW IT WORKS:
Multiple mirrors

Modern reflecting telescopes often use an array of several smaller mirrors, or mirrors made up of several identical units. The separate mirrors work together like a single, very large mirror. Astronomers use computers to keep the mirrors very accurately positioned.

Telescopes in space

The blanket of air that surrounds the Earth is known as the **atmosphere**. It keeps the planet warm, gives us air to breathe and protects us from harmful rays. But for astronomers it is a nuisance. The atmosphere gets in the way of clear observations, and stops some kinds of light from reaching the Earth at all. For the best possible view of the Universe, you need a telescope in space.

First into space

In the 1960s, the US space agency, **NASA**, made plans for a large telescope in space. They decided to call it the Hubble Space Telescope (HST). Construction began in 1977, but the HST was not ready until 1985. The launch was delayed until 1990, and then astronomers found that there was a problem with the telescope's mirror, and it did not focus properly!

In 1993 astronauts flew out to the HST and repaired it. Since then it has been sending back incredible pictures of space, from the nearest planets to **galaxies** right at the edge of the known Universe.

The Sun and the stars we see in the sky are part of the same galaxy – a huge spiral of stars all moving together. This HST image shows another galaxy. Galaxies can be different shapes, but this one is similar to ours.

How the HST works

The HST orbits at around 580 kilometres (360 miles) above Earth. It is about the size of a single-decker bus. Sticking out from the sides of the telescope are large solar panels. These provide the electricity to power the telescope.

Hubble is controlled from the ground, using radio signals. Astronomers can point it at any part of the sky. Scientists who want to use the HST book time on the telescope. You can see many of the photos taken by HST by going to the gallery on the Hubble website (http://hubblesite.org).

This view of the HST was taken from the space shuttle. The silver cylinder is the telescope itself. In the foreground are the solar panels.

Invisible light

The light that we see from stars is only a small part of the energy that they produce. This energy is given off as **radiation** – rays of energy. Light is one kind of radiation, but there are many other kinds that we cannot see.

From radio waves to gamma rays

Different kinds of radiation have different amounts of energy. **Radio waves** have the lowest energy, while X-rays and gamma rays are very high-energy types of radiation. Light is somewhere in the middle of the whole range. Heat rays are known as **infra-red** radiation. They have slightly less energy than light rays. **Ultraviolet** radiation has slightly more energy than visible light.

These two pictures of the Moon are an ultraviolet image (left) and a visible light image (right). They show quite similar views, but some of the areas of high ground that are bright in visible light are dark in the ultraviolet image.

Seeing invisible light

Once astronomers began to learn about different kinds of radiation, they started to wonder: what would the stars look like if we could see the other kinds of radiation they give off?

In the 20th century, it became possible to build different types of telescope, which could "see" different kinds of radiation. Using these telescopes, astronomers have learned all kinds of new things about the stars. For instance, astronomers can now "see" stars that are hidden behind thick clouds. They have also found that some "stars" are not stars at all, but are very distant galaxies producing huge amounts of energy.

HOT NEWS:
The first "invisible light"

Sir William Herschel was an astronomer, but he was also interested in other kinds of science. In 1800 he did an experiment to see if different colours of light had different temperatures. He passed sunlight through a prism, which split the white light into a spectrum (a rainbow). He measured the temperature of each colour using thermometers, and found that the temperature increased from blue to red. Herschel then measured the temperature just past the red end of the spectrum, where there was no visible light. He found that the temperature here was even higher. Herschel realized that there must be some kind of "invisible" light in this area. We now call it infra-red radiation. Infra-red was the first kind of invisible radiation to be discovered.

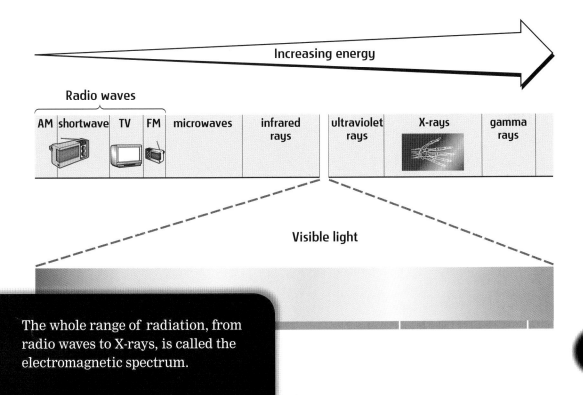

The whole range of radiation, from radio waves to X-rays, is called the electromagnetic spectrum.

Radio telescopes

In the 1930s, the Bell telephone company in the United Sates wanted to use radio waves to send telephone calls across the Atlantic. They asked an engineer called Karl Jansky to check if there was any radio "static" that would interfere with the phone calls. Jansky built a large radio antenna, and recorded the radio signals it picked up. He found that thunderstorms produced static, but otherwise there was only a faint background "hiss".

The hiss puzzled Jansky. At first he thought it was caused by the Sun. But eventually he discovered that the source was actually near the centre of the Milky Way (our galaxy). He had accidentally made the first radio telescope.

Giant dishes

Astronomers did not use Jansky's discovery straight away. But after World War II, they began to build **satellite** dishes to detect radio signals from space. A satellite is anything that orbits the Earth or another planet. The dishes of radio telescopes are designed to collect and focus radio waves, just as curved mirrors collect and focus light waves. But radio waves are much longer than light waves, so the dishes needed to be much bigger.

In the 1950s and 1960s, astronomers worked out ways to link together whole arrays of radio dishes, so that they worked together like one giant telescope. These giant arrays made it possible to build radio telescopes that are more powerful than the best optical telescopes (ones that use light).

The dish of a radio telescope picks up faint radio signals from space, and focuses them on a very sensitive detector. These radio dishes are part of a large array.

What do radio telescopes "see"?

Radio telescopes and optical telescopes each "notice" different things. A bright star might hardly be visible through a radio telescope, but can be clearly seen through an optical one. Some **neutron stars** give out no light, but have a very strong radio signal.

Biography:
Grote Reber

Grote Reber was interested in anything to do with radios. When he learned of Jansky's discoveries, he built a radio telescope in his back yard and began studying the skies. Between 1938 and 1943, Reber made the first radio wave maps of the sky. Like Jansky, he found that the brightest area was near the centre of the Milky Way. After World War II, astronomers in many countries began building bigger and better radio telescopes to study Reber's discoveries.

This radio image shows a neutron star. Neutron stars are the remains of large stars that have exploded. They were first discovered using radio telescopes.

Seeing through the clouds

Some parts of space are hidden by vast clouds of gas and dust. What is inside these clouds? What is behind them?

Picking up infra-red

One way to find out is to use an infra-red telescope. An infra-red telescope picks up heat rays. It can "see" through clouds that block the view in visible light. On Earth it is difficult to pick up the faint infra-red signals from the stars, because the atmosphere blocks infra-red radiation. So infra-red telescopes have to be sent out into space.

To pick up distant heat rays, infra-red telescopes have to be cooled to nearly minus 273 °C (minus 459°F). They also need a sunshield to block out infra-red radiation from the Sun.

Infra-red telescopes give astronomers all sorts of useful information. They can detect new planets forming around other stars. They can reveal the formation of stars in the heart of dust clouds. They can also look into the cloudy centres of distant galaxies.

This nebula is 5400 light years away in the **constellation** Sagittarius. Scientists used an infra-red telescope to view stars forming in the nebula.

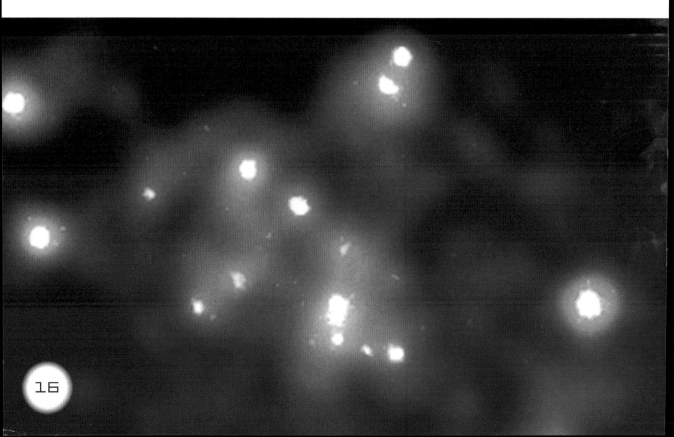

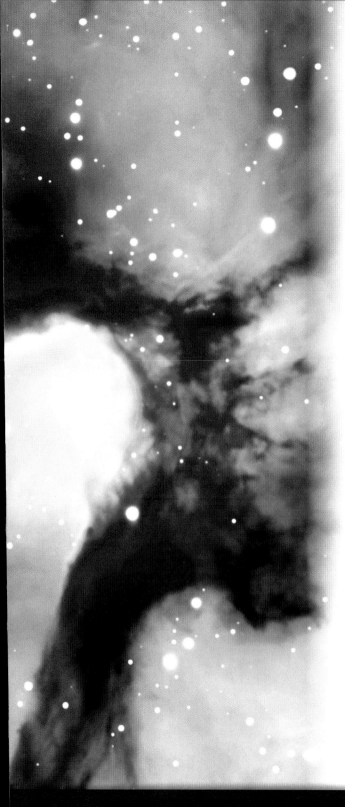

High-energy telescopes

X-rays are high-energy types of radiation. High-energy radiation is produced when something is giving off a lot of energy. So X-ray telescopes detect violent events taking place in space. Star explosions, neutron stars, and **black holes** all produce large amounts of X-ray radiation.

If X-rays rays hit a mirror head-on, they plough straight into it instead of bouncing off. In order to focus these high-energy rays, astronomers have to make sure they just graze the surface of the mirror and bounce off. So the mirror of an X-ray telescope is shaped like half a barrel, rather than like the mirror of a light telescope.

HOW IT WORKS:
Detecting the remains of stars

Stars last for millions or billions of years, but eventually they die. When large stars die, the outer parts explode. The inner part of the star collapses to form a small, incredibly heavy object called a neutron star. If the star is even bigger, when it collapses it forms an even smaller object, known as a black hole. A black hole's gravity is enormously strong. It sucks in anything that comes close. When material is sucked into a black hole, it gets incredibly hot and gives off X-rays.

Most stars begin their lives surrounded by clouds of dust. But an infra-red telescope can see through the dust clouds to the stars inside. This image shows more than 300 newborn stars.

Rockets and space probes

"Ten, nine, eight, seven, six, five, four, three, two, one ... LIFT OFF!" Clouds, smoke, and flame shoot out of the bottom of the rocket, and it slowly climbs into the air. As it climbs, it gets faster and faster. Soon it is just a dot in the sky.

Telescopes let us look at the stars, but they don't help us to travel into space. To do that, we need rockets.

Rocket power

A rocket motor is similar to a jet engine. Both engines burn fuel in a **combustion chamber**. This produces lots of hot gases, which shoot out of the engine at high speed.

A jet engine burns fuel using oxygen, which it gets from the air. Out in space there is no air, so a jet engine cannot work. Rockets get round this problem by carrying a supply of oxygen as well as fuel.

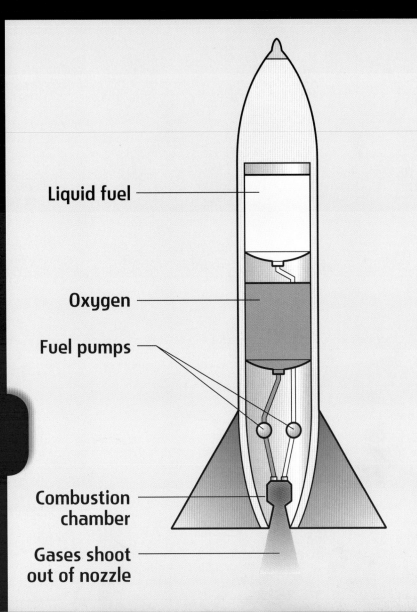

Liquid fuel

Oxygen

Fuel pumps

Combustion chamber

Gases shoot out of nozzle

This shows how a liquid-fuel rocket motor works.

Rocket history

The Chinese were the first people to make rockets. In the 13th century, they developed rocket-powered "arrows of flying fire" to use in battle.

In 1898 a Russian scientist called Konstantin Tsiolkovsy suggested that rockets could be used to explore space. He also suggested using liquid fuel for rocket motors. In the 1920s American Robert Goddard carried out many experiments with liquid-fuelled rockets. He also worked out ways to control their flight.

During World War II a team of scientists in Germany built a powerful rocket weapon called the V-2. This rocket could fly long distances, and exploded when it hit the ground. It was the first guided **missile**. After the war, rockets similar to the V-2 were built for space exploration.

HOW IT WORKS:
Rocket motors

Many rockets have a tank of oxygen and a tank of **hydrogen**. Oxygen and hydrogen are both gases, but in a rocket they are cooled and compressed (squashed) to make them liquid. The hydrogen and oxygen mix in a combustion chamber, and the mixture explodes. The hot gases fly out of a nozzle at the back of the rocket, and push the spacecraft forwards.

This Delta rocket was used to launch the NEAR-Shoemaker probe in 1995 (see page 25).

Satellites and space probes

In October 1957, a Russian rocket made the first real trip into space. It was carrying a small metal sphere about the size of a basketball. The metal ball was *Sputnik 1*, the world's first artificial satellite. *Sputnik 1* orbited the Earth for several months, sending a regular "beep beep" radio signal as it flew.

Orbiting the Earth

Since Sputnik, many other artificial satellites have been launched into space. Many of them are not concerned with space exploration. They do things like help predict the weather, or send TV and telephone messages round the world. However, there are also scientific satellites that take measurements of things such as **magnetic fields** and **cosmic radiation**. There are also several space telescopes, such as the Hubble Space Telescope (see pages 10–11) and the Chandra X-ray Observatory.

Satellites collect information about other planets. This image of the surface of Venus has been created using data gathered by the *Magellan* probe.

Space probes

Many unmanned spacecraft have been sent to explore beyond Earth's orbit. These spacecraft are called space probes. The first was *Luna 1*, which passed close to the Moon in 1959. Since then, space probes have visited every planet in our Solar System except for Pluto. Some have studied one planet in detail. For instance, the *Magellan* space probe travelled to Venus in 1990 and orbited the planet for four years. During that time it took detailed **radar** photos of almost the whole planet.

Other space probes have made very long journeys and visited several planets. The two Voyager space probes (*Voyagers I* and *II*) were launched in the 1970s. Between them they visited Jupiter, Saturn, Uranus, and Neptune. Both probes have now left the Solar System. They continue to send messages back to Earth as they fly on towards the stars.

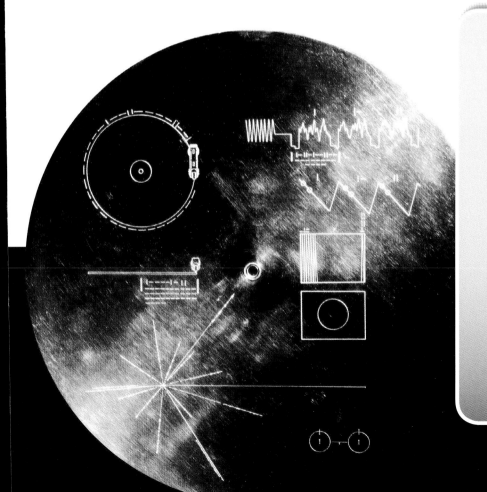

HOT NEWS:
Messages for aliens?

NASA estimates that the *Voyager* probes will run out of power in about 2020. But they will probably carry on travelling through space for many years after that. If aliens were to pick up one of the probes deep in space, they would find a message from Earth on board. Each probe carries a gold record (left). On the record there are sounds, music and pictures showing life on Earth.

Landing on other planets

Looking at a planet from space can give us a lot of information, but to really know what it is like you have to land there. So some space probes have been designed to land on other planets.

Coming in to land

Space probes designed to land are more complicated than other space probes. Part of the probe is the "mother ship", which actually flies to the new planet. It carries cameras and other instruments to send back information about the planet from space. Once in orbit around the planet, the mother ship releases a small landing pod. When it lands, the pod opens up so that the instruments on board can send back information to Earth.

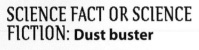
SCIENCE FACT OR SCIENCE FICTION: Dust buster

Before humans went to the Moon, scientists thought that the whole surface of the Moon might be covered in a thick layer of dust. This would have made landing very difficult. The *Luna 9* probe in 1966 opened up the way for humans to visit the Moon. It showed that the Moon's surface was hard and had only a thin covering of dust.

This picture shows the roving robot *Spirit*, which explored the surface of Mars.

Lander history

The first landing probe was a Russian probe called *Luna 9*. It made a soft landing on the Moon in 1966. Another Russian probe, *Venera 7*, reached Venus in 1970. It was designed to study the atmosphere, but it also landed and sent back weak messages. Later, other *Venera* probes sent back photos of the planet's surface.

More recent landing probes have done more than just land on the surface. The space probes *Viking I* and *Viking II* had robot arms that picked up samples of the Martian soil and tested it for signs of life. Two more recent probes were the *Mars Exploration Rovers A* and *B*. Both landed on Mars in 2003. Each probe carried a roving robot on board, one called *Spirit* and the other called *Opportunity*. These two robots are still moving about on the planet's surface and sending back information.

In 2004 the *Cassini* space probe arrived at the planet Saturn. Six months later it sent a small probe called *Huygens* down onto the surface of Titan, Saturn's biggest moon. This artwork was based on the photos taken by *Huygens* on Titan.

Probing the limits

Space probes have investigated other objects besides moons and planets. Several space probes have studied the Sun, while others have travelled to visit **asteroids** and **comets**.

Circling the Sun

Two space probes, called *Wind* and *Ace*, are circling the Sun at the same speed as the Earth. They are studying something called the solar wind. Every second, the Sun throws out billions and billions of very tiny particles, smaller than **atoms**. These particles shoot away from the Sun at very high speeds. This stream of particles is the solar wind. The *Ace* and *Wind* probes have detectors that measure the strength of the solar wind, and the particles that are in it.

Space probes are controlled from a mission control centre on Earth. The controllers can send radio signals to the probe to check that everything is working properly, or to fire the probe's engines. The probe sends information from its instruments back to Earth.

This photo of the asteroid Eros was taken by the NEAR-Shoemaker probe.

Rocks in space

Other probes have visited asteroids, which are large rocks orbiting the Sun. In 2000, the NEAR-Shoemaker probe met up with an asteroid called Eros about 316 million kilometres (196 million miles) from Earth. It orbited the asteroid for a year, then landed on it. Another probe called *Muses-C* is on its way to a different asteroid. The plan is for it to take a sample of rock from the asteroid and bring it back to Earth.

Probing comets

A comet is a huge ball of rock and ice that spends most of its time at the edges of the Solar System. But once in a while the comet gets quite close to the Sun. When this happens, some of the comet melts, and forms a long "tail" of gas and dust.

In 2004, the space probe *Stardust* flew through the tail of a comet and collected some gas and dust from it. *Stardust* is now on its way back to Earth. Then in 2005 another probe, *Deep Impact*, crash-landed on a comet. The space probe *Rosetta* will soft-land on a comet in 2014.

Putting people in space

Sending probes into space is one thing. Sending astronauts up in a rocket is something else. There are so many extra things to worry about. People need air to breathe, but there is no air in space. We cannot get too hot or too cold, but space gets very hot when the Sun is shining on you, and very cold when it is not. We need food and water, but there is no food in space, and no water. Spacecraft designed to carry humans into space have to deal with all these problems, and many others.

Solving the problems

Space scientists have managed to solve most of the problems of getting people into space. The spacecraft is sealed so that it is airtight, and it is kept full of air so that the astronauts can breathe. The spacecraft is also protected from harmful radiation such as X-rays, which could injure the astronauts. **Insulation** keeps out the worst of the heat and the cold, and the spacecraft is stocked up with plenty of food and water.

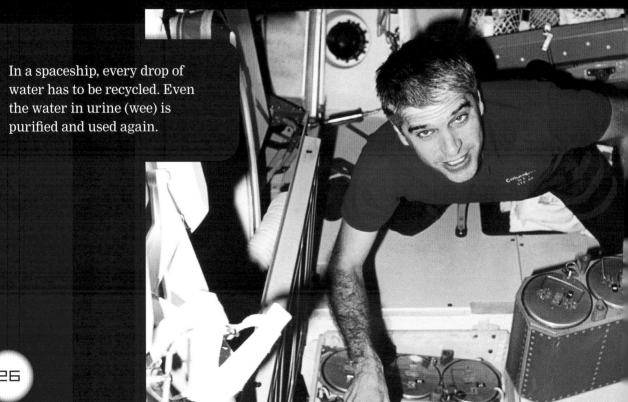

In a spaceship, every drop of water has to be recycled. Even the water in urine (wee) is purified and used again.

Too much weight

One unsolved problem is that all the extra protection and equipment adds weight. A spacecraft designed to carry people is far heavier than one carrying a robot space probe. It also needs rockets that are many times more powerful in order to get into space. So everything possible has to be done to save weight. The spacecraft and all the equipment in it are built of the lightest materials available. Food is dried or concentrated, to make it lighter. And everything is recycled or reused that can be.

HOW IT WORKS:
Life support in a suit

If astronauts have to go outside the spacecraft, they wear a spacesuit. This has to protect the astronaut in the same way that the spacecraft does. The suit has an air supply, built-in heating and cooling, and protection from harmful rays. For walks in space, the suit also has a jet pack for moving around and a safety line to stop the astronaut from losing touch with the spacecraft.

One job of a spacesuit is to protect an astronaut from temperature extremes. The side of the suit facing the Sun may get hotter than boiling water, while in the shadow, it may be as cold as minus 157 °C (minus 251°F).

Early flights

On 12 April 1961 the Russian astronaut Yuri Gagarin climbed into a small, round capsule on top of the *Vostok 1* rocket. The rocket roared off the launch pad and flew into space. The space capsule did a complete orbit of the Earth, travelling at 27,000 kilometres per hour (17,000 miles per hour). It was the first ever human space flight.

The space race

Yuri Gagarin's flight was part of a "space race" between the USA and Russia. In 1961 Russia was well ahead in the race and it was another year before John Glenn became the first US astronaut to circle the Earth. But soon after Gagarin's flight, President Kennedy of the USA made an announcement. He promised that the US would land an astronaut on the Moon within the next ten years.

US astronauts flew many missions to test out every stage of a possible Moon flight. Astronauts took space walks outside the capsule, to test out spacesuits and other equipment. They also travelled to the Moon without landing, to rehearse all the details of the Moon flight.

By 1969, the USA was ready to send astronauts to the Moon.

Yuri Gagarin joined the Russian air force in 1955. Four years later he began his training as a cosmonaut.

HOW IT WORKS:
Launch vehicles and capsules

Most space rockets have two parts, the launch vehicle and the space capsule. The launch vehicle is a huge rocket with enough power to blast one or more people into space. The capsule is a small cabin where the astronauts sit.

The launch rocket usually has two or three different stages (sections). As the fuel in each stage is used up, the stage drops off, so as to save weight. Eventually only the capsule is left.

At the end of the flight the capsule falls back to Earth. Parachutes open to slow it down as it gets close to the ground.

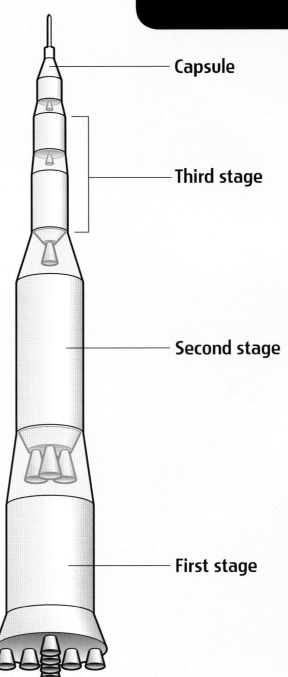

Capsule

Third stage

Second stage

First stage

HOT NEWS:

Since 1961 there have been many space flights. However, until recently all of the spacecraft had been built for **governments.** Then in 2004, a privately built spacecraft travelled into space for the first time. Mike Melvill was the pilot of the rocket *SpaceShipOne*. It was lifted high into the atmosphere by a carrier aircraft. Once it was set free, the rocket flew to a height of 100 kilometres (62 miles). It stayed in space for about three minutes.

Trips to the Moon

On 20 July 1969, people all over the world gathered round their television sets. The pictures they were watching were grainy and black and white. The sound was fuzzy and hard to understand. But nobody minded. They were watching the first astronauts on the Moon.

Lift-off!

The *Apollo 11* Moon mission took off on 16 July. The rocket carried the space capsule *Columbia*, with three astronauts on board: Neil Armstrong, Buzz Aldrin, and Michael Collins.

The first two stages of the rocket took *Columbia* into orbit. Then the third stage fired and the spacecraft **accelerated** to almost 40,000 km/h (25,000 mph). This was fast enough to escape Earth's gravity. *Apollo* was on its way to the Moon.

Reaching the Moon

The trip to the Moon took about 77 hours. Once *Columbia* reached Moon orbit, Armstrong and Aldrin climbed into *Eagle*, a small Moon lander. Michael Collins stayed on *Columbia*, while *Eagle* landed on the Moon.

This photo shows the Moonlander in the centre and the lunar roving vehicle on the right.

Later missions

The *Apollo 11* mission was a great success. It was the first of six Moon landings. On the last three missions, the astronauts stayed on the Moon for three days, setting up all kinds of scientific experiments. They were able to travel much further because they had transport in the form of an electric car called the lunar roving vehicle.

Sending astronauts to the Moon was very expensive, and after a few Moon missions, people began to lose interest. So in 1972, after the *Apollo 17* mission, the trips to the Moon ended.

SCIENCE FACT OR SCIENCE FICTION:
Other ways to the Moon?

In the 19th century, writers wrote stories about trips to the Moon. In *From the Earth to the Moon*, Jules Verne's space travellers are fired at the Moon from a giant gun. In *The First Men on the Moon* by H. G. Wells, the astronauts travel in a spacecraft painted with anti-gravity paint.

Jules Verne's ideas were not as silly as they might sound. His space capsule was about the same size and weight as the Apollo's space capsule, *Columbia*, and it flew at the right speed to reach the Moon. H. G. Wells's anti-gravity idea is less likely. There has been some research into anti-gravity, but there is no evidence that it exists.

The Saturn 5 rocket was the launch vehicle for the Moon missions. It was the most powerful rocket yet built.

The Space Shuttle

After the Moon missions, NASA (the US space agency) concentrated on building a new kind of spacecraft. The Space Shuttle looked more like a large plane than a rocket.

Reusable spacecraft

Until Space Shuttles were built, most of a rocket ended up as scrap metal within minutes of lift-off. The main part of each rocket was the launch vehicle, which was thrown away during the climb into space.

Space Shuttles, however, are mostly reusable. The main part of the Shuttle is the orbiter. This is used again and again. At launch, there are two other parts to the Shuttle: a giant fuel tank and two booster rockets. The booster rockets are used up first, and drop away from the Shuttle. However, they are recovered after the flight and used again. The only part of the Shuttle that is not used again is the main fuel tank. This is discarded just before the Shuttle goes into orbit.

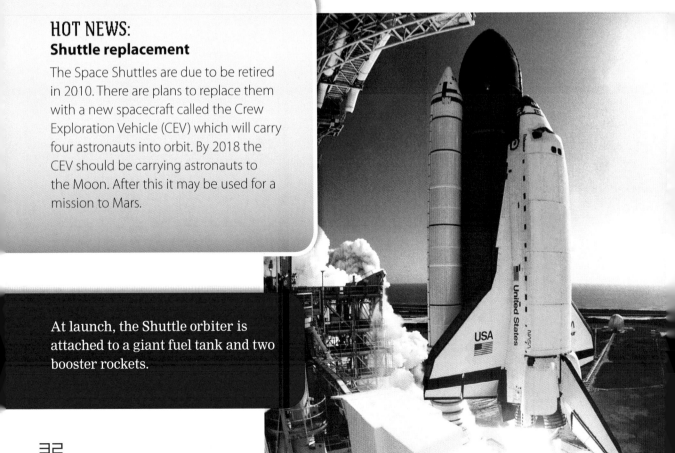

HOT NEWS:
Shuttle replacement

The Space Shuttles are due to be retired in 2010. There are plans to replace them with a new spacecraft called the Crew Exploration Vehicle (CEV) which will carry four astronauts into orbit. By 2018 the CEV should be carrying astronauts to the Moon. After this it may be used for a mission to Mars.

At launch, the Shuttle orbiter is attached to a giant fuel tank and two booster rockets.

Cargo ship

The Space Shuttle is designed for carrying cargo into space. Its large cargo bay has been used to carry satellites, scientific instruments and parts of space stations (see pages 34–35). The Shuttle *Discovery* lifted the Hubble Space Telescope into orbit in 1990.

The Shuttle can only reach an orbit of about 300 to 400 kilometres (185 to 250 miles) above Earth. However, some satellites orbit much higher than this. In these cases the satellite has a booster rocket attached, which takes it higher than the Shuttle's orbit.

The astronauts on the Space Shuttle have an amazing view as they orbit the Earth.

Space stations

Travelling through space is one thing. But what about living in space? Space stations allow astronauts to live and work in space. There have been space stations above the Earth since the 1970s.

Early space stations

The very first space station, the Russian *Salyut 1*, was launched in 1971. It was followed by a series of other Russian space stations during the 1970s. A US space station called *Skylab* was also used briefly during 1973 and 1974.

Mir

The most successful Russian space station was called *Mir*. The first part of *Mir* was launched in 1986, and new parts were added gradually over the next ten years. It was allowed to fall out of orbit in 2001.

Mir was the first really successful space laboratory. From 1986 to 1999, there were astronauts on board nearly all the time. Scientists from many different countries visited the space station. They studied the effects of life in low gravity, the nature of space, and many other subjects.

The *Mir* space station in orbit above the Earth.

The ISS

Since 1998 a new space station has been taking shape above Earth. This is the *International Space Station (ISS)*. The *ISS* is already bigger than a three-bedroom house. When it is finished, it will be over four times bigger than *Mir*.

As with *Mir*, the *ISS* is being used for many scientific experiments. At the moment many of these are concerned with making it possible to live for long periods in space. Can we grow plants in space and use them for food? How can we stop muscles and bones from wasting away in the low gravity of space? Can we protect astronauts from high-energy radiation for long periods of time? These are just some of the questions experiments on the *ISS* are trying to answer.

TRY IT YOURSELF: Find the ISS

The *ISS* is sometimes visible in the sky as a bright "star". If you go to the website Heavens Above (http://www.heavens-above.com/) and register, you can find out if the ISS will be visible from where you are in the next ten days.

The *ISS* regularly receives supplies from Earth. These are transported by automatic spacecraft that do not have any astronauts on board.

A mission to Mars?

For many years, scientists have been particularly interested in the planet Mars. This is because conditions on Mars are more like those on Earth than on any other planet in our Solar System. There was probably water on Mars in the past. Water is essential for living things, so there may once have been life there.

A long trip

Many space probes have been sent to Mars in the last 30 years. Scientists know a huge amount about the planet. But the ultimate goal would be for humans to travel to Mars. A trip to Mars would be more difficult than travelling to the Moon. A round trip to Mars would take two years, rather than four days for a Moon trip. Scientists in several countries are working on plans for a trip to Mars in about 2030.

Pictures of the surface of Mars show strong evidence that there was once water. There are dried up river valleys and evidence of sudden floods.

Return to the Moon

Before travelling to Mars, the plan is to return to the Moon and set up bases there. Scientists will use the Moon missions to test out the spacecraft and other equipment. Advances in technology since the 1960s mean that it is cheaper to fly to the Moon now than it was then.

The next stage could be to send robot spacecraft to Mars. These spacecraft could carry heavy supplies needed for the Mars trip. Finally, humans will travel to Mars.

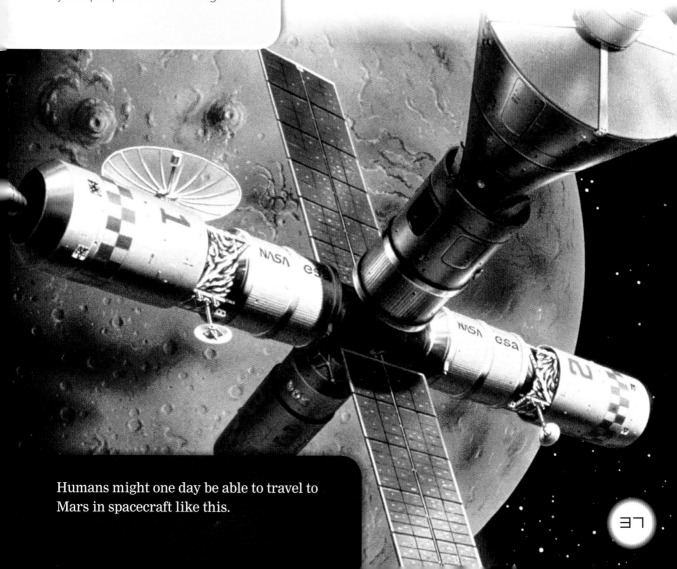

Humans might one day be able to travel to Mars in spacecraft like this.

Work in progress

A space mission to Mars might last two years. A trip this long creates all sorts of problems that don't come up on shorter trips. Scientists are finding interesting answers to these problems.

Wasting away

On a long mission astronauts would live in zero gravity (be weightless) for many months. This causes the bones and muscles in the body to become very weak. They lose strength because the body does not have to support itself against gravity.

One solution to this problem would be to create artificial gravity on the spacecraft. When you spin around on a fairground ride, you get pressed against the outside. The spinning creates a kind of artificial gravity. Scientists are planning to build spacecraft that spin to create artificial gravity on board ship.

Exercise helps to stop muscles and bones becoming too weak in zero gravity. This experiment is testing the effects of exercise in space.

This is one idea of what a space base on Mars might look like.

Dangerous rays

The Sun produces ultraviolet light, X-rays and other kinds of radiation that can cause cancer and other diseases. On Earth, the atmosphere protects us from much of this radiation. But in space we need other kinds of protection.

The metal skin of a spacecraft does not give much protection against harmful radiation. However, scientists have found that materials containing lots of hydrogen, such as water and plastics, are good at stopping harmful rays. It may be possible to use the spacecraft's water supplies, perhaps kept in plastic tanks, to protect the crew of a spacecraft from radiation.

Going faster

If spacecraft could travel faster, this would cut the amount of time astronauts spend in space. The ion drive used on the *Deep Space 1* probe (see the box on page 25) is not powerful enough to use on a manned mission. However, scientists are working on combining this drive with a **nuclear power plant**. With a motor of this kind, a spacecraft could get to Mars in just three months.

Is there anyone out there?

Scientists want to travel to Mars to see if they can find out whether there was once life there. But what about beyond our Solar System? Perhaps there is life somewhere else. There are billions of stars in our galaxy, and billions of other galaxies besides ours. Perhaps one of these stars has a planet that is similar to Earth. And on this planet there might be intelligent living things.

Other planets

Astronomers have known about the nine planets of our Solar System for many years. But in the past ten years or so they have also discovered planets orbiting around other stars. Astronomers found the first one in 1995. It is about half the size of Jupiter, and orbiting very close to a star called 51 Pegasi. The planet has been named Bellerophon.

Since this first discovery, over 150 planets have been found travelling round other stars. Many of them are giant gas planets orbiting very close to their sun, as with Bellerophon. However, more recently a few smaller, rocky planets more like Earth have been found. One of these is about 15 light years from Earth, orbiting the star Gliese 876. Who knows? Maybe in the future we will find the first ever life on this planet.

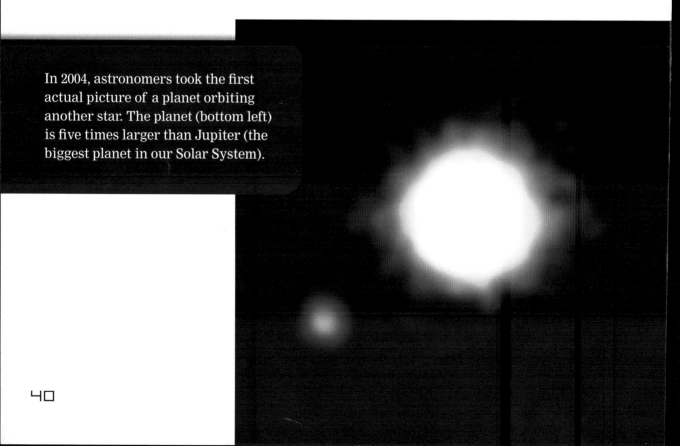

In 2004, astronomers took the first actual picture of a planet orbiting another star. The planet (bottom left) is five times larger than Jupiter (the biggest planet in our Solar System).

TRY IT YOURSELF:
Look for aliens

We cannot yet travel to planets around other stars, but perhaps if there are aliens out there we can find them another way. One scientific project, called SETI@home, searches for radio signals from **extraterrestrial** living things (aliens from another planet). It does this using millions of computers connected to the Internet.

The SETI website (http://setiathome.ssl.berkeley.edu/) has a special screensaver program that anyone can download onto their computer. It starts up when your computer is running but you are not using it. It shuts down as soon as you return to work. The screensaver program looks through the radio signals collected by the world's largest radio telescope. It searches for radio messages that could have been sent by aliens.

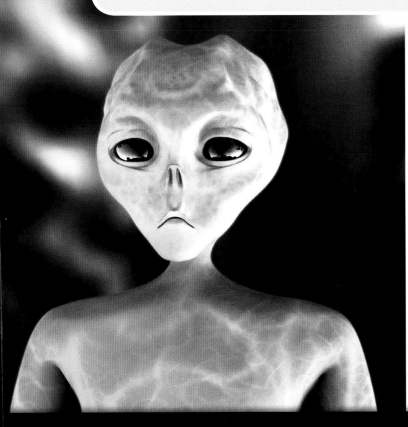

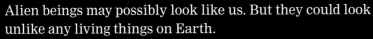

Alien beings may possibly look like us. But they could look unlike any living things on Earth.

Flights to the stars?

What would we need in order to travel to the stars? We would need to travel very fast, and we would need to use much less fuel than a normal rocket does. At the speed of our fastest rockets, the trip to the nearest stars would take about 100,000 years. If we wanted to do the trip more quickly, the problem would be fuel. With a normal rocket motor, the fuel we would need would weigh more than the entire Universe!

Sails and sun-power

If we can't use rockets to get to the stars, what else might work? Scientists have some ideas. One is to use something called a solar sail. This is an enormous, very thin, very light "sail" with a shiny surface. It would work like a sail on a boat, but the wind that pushed it along would be light, rather than moving air. The push of a light beam is very, very tiny. But with a big enough sail, and the light pushing it for long enough, it could reach high speeds. *Cosmos-1* was a test solar sail. It was launched in June 2005, but with limited success.

Another idea is to use a rocket powered by nuclear fusion. This is the same process that makes the Sun shine. The fuel for nuclear fusion is the gas hydrogen. There are tiny amounts of hydrogen floating in space. The fusion rocket would suck up the hydrogen from space as it travelled, and use it to power the rocket motor.

SCIENCE FACT OR SCIENCE FICTION:
Wormholes in space

In science fiction movies, spaceships can travel huge distances very quickly. In the far future, scientists think we might be able to do the same, using so-called "wormholes". These are holes through space and time itself – with one end in one part of space, and the other end somewhere else entirely. Scientists think that wormholes form naturally, but they last only a fraction of a second. If we could make wormholes, and keep them open, then we could travel across the Universe!

The Pleiades are 425 years away, even at the speed of light. Could we find a way to get there?

Not so far away

Today, star travel seems like a fantasy. But 100 years ago, travelling to the Moon was an impossible dream. So who knows? Maybe in 100 years time we will be heading for the stars.

Timeline of space travel

1608 Hans Lippershey and others in the Netherlands make the first telescopes.

1609 The Italian scientist Galileo sees the moons of Jupiter with a telescope.

1668 Isaac Newton builds a reflecting telescope.

1930s Grote Reber builds the first radio telescope.

1957 *Sputnik 1* is the first human-made object to orbit the Earth.

1961 Russian Yuri Gagarin orbits the Earth in the rocket *Vostok 1*. He is the first astronaut in space.

1963 Russian Valenta Tereshkova is the first woman in space. She orbits the Earth 48 times.

1966 *Luna 9* is the first spacecraft to soft-land on the Moon.

1969 Neil Armstrong and Edwin Aldrin, Jr. make the first manned landing on the Moon in *Apollo 11*.

1971 *Mariner 9* space probe orbits Mars. It is the first spacecraft to orbit another planet.

1977 *Voyager 1* and *Voyager 2* space probes leave Earth to meet up with Jupiter in 1979 and Saturn in 1980.

1981 The first manned mission of the Space Shuttle is launched.

1986 The Space Shuttle *Challenger* explodes shortly after lift-off.

1986 The core unit of Soviet space station *Mir* is launched.

1990 The Hubble Space Telescope (HST) is launched, but its main mirror is out of focus.

1993 Space Shuttle *Endeavour* flies to the HST and repairs the main mirror.

1995 Cosmonaut Valeri Polyakov returns to Earth after a 438-day stay in space – the longest ever.

1996 NEAR-Shoemaker probe reaches the asteroid Eros in 2000 and lands on it in 2001.

1997 The space probe *Cassini/Huygens* is launched. *Cassini* arrives at Saturn in 2004. It drops a separate probe, *Huygens*, onto the surface of Saturn's largest moon, Titan.

1998 NASA launches *Deep Space 1*, the first space probe driven by an ion engine.

1999 The Chandra X-Ray Observatory is carried into orbit.

2001 American businessman Dennis Tito becomes the first tourist to fly into space.

2004 *SpaceShipOne* is the first private spacecraft to fly a human into space.

Travel times to planets and stars

The fastest speed that a rocket can travel is about 40,000 km/h (25,000 mph). This table shows how long it would take to travel to other planets and to the stars at this speed.

Destination	Travel time (one way)
Moon	half a day
Sun	6 months
Mars	8 months
Pluto (farthest planet)	14 years
Proxima centauri (nearest star)	100,000 years

Glossary

accelerate to go faster

ancestors people from the past

asteroid a piece of rock, smaller than a planet, orbiting the Sun

atmosphere the layer of air that surrounds the Earth

atoms the tiny particles that everything is made of

black hole very tiny, very dense object that has such strong gravity that not even light can escape from it

combustion chamber closed container in an engine or motor where fuel burns

comet lump of ice and rock that travels in a huge orbit around the Sun

constellation pattern of stars in the night sky

cosmic radiation rays of very high-energy radiation that travel through space

extraterrestrial something from outside the Earth

focus bring together

galaxy an "island" in space of millions or billions of stars

hydrogen the lightest gas, and the main material that stars are made of

infra-red kind of radiation that has slightly less energy than visible light

insulation something that stops heat from escaping

magnetic field the area around any magnet where it affects iron or other magnetic material

missile rocket with a warhead made from high explosive

NASA (National Aeronautics and Science Administration) the US space agency

neutron star small, very dense lump of material left after a supernova (huge explosion of a dying star)

nuclear power plant machine that produces energy (usually electricity) from nuclear reactions (usually splitting atoms)

orbit to go around

prism specially shaped piece of glass (usually pyramid-shaped) that is used to split light

radar device that "sees" by sending out radio waves and then picking up the echoes as they bounce off objects

radiation light, or rays that are similar to light but invisible

radio waves kind of low-energy radiation

satellite something that orbits the Earth or another planet

Solar System the Sun and the nine planets and other objects that orbit around it

spectroscope instrument for splitting light into a spectrum (range) of colours

ultraviolet kind of radiation that has slightly more energy than visible light

Further information

Books

Encyclopedia of Space, Heather Couper and Nigel Henbest (Dorling Kindersley, 2003)

How to Get to the Moon, Hazel Richardson (Oxford University Press, 1999)

Space Odyssey: Voyage to the Planets Mission Report, Steve Cole (Dorling Kindersley, 2004)

Telescopes and Observatories, Heather Couper and Nigel Henbest (Franklin Watts, 1987)

Places to visit

Royal Observatory
Greenwich
London
SE10 9NF
UK
+44 (0)20 8312 6565
www.rog.nmm.ac.uk/

Siding Spring Observatory
Coonabarabran
National Park Road
New South Wales
Australia
+64 (0)2 68-426211
www.sidingspringexploratory.com.au

Websites

Space and beyond *http://kids.msfc.nasa.gov/Space/*
A website about stars, black holes, quasars and other space stuff, from NASA. Also includes Astronomy Picture of the Day.

Hubble gallery *http://hubblesite.org/gallery/*
A gallery of pictures and movies from the Hubble Space Telescope.

Rockets and airplanes *http://kids.msfc.nasa.gov/Rockets/*
A NASA website about the Space Shuttle, the ISS, space probes, and other spacecraft.

SETI@home *http://setiathome.ssl.berkeley.edu/*
Download a screensaver to help look for aliens.

Index

Titles in the *Stargazers' Guides* series include:

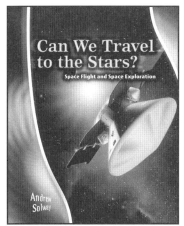

Hardback   0 431 18190 X

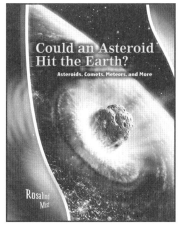

Hardback   0 431 18188 8

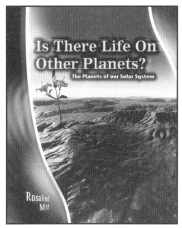

Hardback   0 431 18187 X

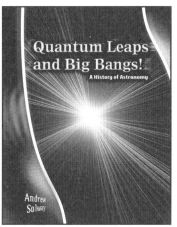

Hardback   0 431 18191 8

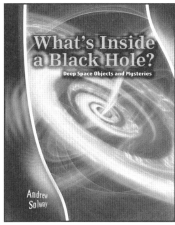

Hardback   0 431 18189 6

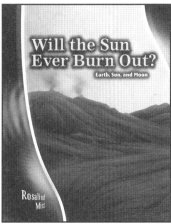

Hardback   0 431 18186 1

Find out about other titles from Heinemann Library on our website www.heinemann.co.uk/library